DAN SEABORN

ONE-MINUTE
DEVOTIONALS
for Couples

Copyright © 1996, 2004 by Winning At Home
All Rights Reserved
Published by Winning At Home
Zeeland, Michigan 49464
Printed in the United States of America
ISBN 0-89827-161-4

Edited by Marilyn Jamieson

Table of Contents

Table of Contents

As Good As It Gets

Song of Songs 4:1

"How beautiful you are, my darling!"

The words spoken by the lover in Song of Songs 4:1-7 are very typical of the culture of that day. At the wedding ceremony, the groom would stand before the host of friends and family gathered there and describe for them his bride using intimate descriptions. He would paint a picture of her loveliness by comparing parts of her body to ordinary things that were both beautiful and worthy. And he would not stop until he had declared his own unending love and devotion using the same kind of language.

When was the last time you described your spouse using words of love and endearment? Times have changed, haven't they? For many of us, the honeymoon is over and the physical attraction we once felt is old news. Marriage is no longer exciting, just comfortable.

How do you renew that bond — that sense of excitement that you used to have? You must not let Satan rob you of the joy and beauty of sexuality in marriage. Make it your top priority to be the best you can be, and then find the words to describe your partner's best qualities. Working together will make your marriage the kind that lasts forever.

Marriage Moments:

- Is your physical relationship as good as it can get?

- What can you do to make it better?

Pray Together

I'm Available

Mark 9:41

"I tell you the truth, anyone who gives you a cup of water
in my name because you belong to Christ will
certainly not lose his reward."

Availability is a key ingredient in any marriage relationship. It is easy to get so caught up in reading the newspaper or cleaning the house that we separate ourselves from each other. We live in the same house, yet we exist in different worlds.

How available are you to your spouse? How willing are you to stop whatever you are doing and listen to your husband recap his day? How often do you turn off the TV and invite your wife to unburden herself within the circle of your arms?

In order to keep your marriage strong, you need to make yourselves available to each other. Go that extra mile, give a cup of water, do the unexpected — make yourself ready and willing to meet the needs of your partner.

Marriage Moments:

- Do you spend time talking each day? How much do you share? How could this improve?

- What issues would you like to talk about that you keep inside?

Pray Together

6

The Benefit of the Doubt

1 Peter 1:22

"Now that you have purified yourselves by obeying the
truth so that you have sincere love for your brother,
love one another deeply, from the heart."

Have you ever criticized your husband for his actions without
understanding why he acted that way? Maybe you've reacted to
something your wife said before giving her a chance to tell the whole
story. Often my wife, Jane, says, "Did you give me the benefit of the
doubt?" I don't like the question, because usually I have made an
assumption too quickly.

Being too quick to make assumptions can cause many problems in
a marriage. The need to always be right must be brought under God's
control if the relationship is to flourish.

Try putting your own thoughts on the back burner and listen to
what your spouse has to say. Respond the way Christ would — with
love and encouragement. See what a difference the benefit of the doubt
can make.

Marriage Moments:

• In your marriage, who most often makes the quick judgmental calls?

• How can you improve in giving each other the benefit of the doubt?

Pray Together

It Is Better To Give

Acts 20:35

"It is more blessed to give than to receive."

My friends, Terry and Nancy, are beautiful examples of stewardship. They continually look for ways to encourage and support other couples. They even teach their children to give their toys to needy kids regularly, not just during the Christmas season. Because of their commitment to giving, the Lord is blessing their lives and their marriage. Their philosophy is, "Everything we own is on loan from God." There are many who say it, but very few who live it.

This philosophy doesn't match the commercialism of our day. However, it corresponds exactly to Christ's challenge to us. He reminds us that blessing can be found in giving, not receiving. Families that are truly happy are those who have found a way to make giving to others a part of their lifestyle.

Marriage Moments:

- Are you good stewards of all God has given you? Who are you influencing by your giving?

- How are you striving to grow in stewardship of your life together?

Pray Together

8

Bologna Moments
Matthew 6:14

"For if you forgive men when they sin against you, your heavenly Father will also forgive you."

A friend shared the following story with me. He and his wife began arguing over the smell of some bologna she had packed in a cooler they had taken on a trip. When their conversation became more heated, their daughter interrupted and pointed out the triteness of the situation. As they stopped and thought about it, they agreed that it truly was silly to allow something so insignificant to become the focus of disagreement. Since then, every time they begin to argue about something unimportant, they call it a "bologna moment," forgive each other and go on.

What a great idea! Recognizing the triteness of "bologna moments" keeps us from building barriers which divide and destroy relationships.

Marriage Moments:
- How often do you experience "bologna moments"?

- Have you let them build up and create barriers in your relationship? If so, pray for forgiveness and go on.

Pray Together

The Buck Stops Here

Proverbs 10:16

"The wages of righteousness bring them life, but the income of the wicked brings them punishment."

It is not uncommon for married couples to experience anxiety and disagreements due to lack of financial planning. Husbands and wives often become very possessive of their money and fail to use it wisely. Soon their debt is overwhelming; they begin to blame each other, and the marriage starts to crumble.

If this scenario in any way reflects your relationship, face reality and stop the slide before your marriage is devastated. Discuss the issue with a counselor or someone you trust to guide you with spiritual and financial wisdom.

Marriage Moments:

- How are you doing financially?

- How can you save and plan better for the future?

Pray Together

Call Waiting

Proverbs 5:15

"Drink water from your own cistern, running water
from your own well."

It is my personal opinion that call-waiting stinks. When I am in the middle of a serious phone conversation, I do not appreciate being interrupted with, "Can you hold a minute? I've got another call." It makes me feel as though what I have to say is not all that important.

The marriage relationship is no place to practice "call waiting" either. Your spouse deserves your full attention when a discussion is taking place. Anything less sends the message that you are not really interested. Many marriages have suffered because one partner — or both — fails to make communication a high priority.

Marriage Moments:

• Do you allow others to grab your attention away from your partner?

• Who or what most often interrupts you? How can you protect yourselves from interruption?

Pray Together

Charming and Noble? Or Chernobyl?

Isaiah 62:5

"As a bridegroom rejoices over his bride,
so will your God rejoice over you."

In their book *Before And After You Fall In Love*, Victoria Brown and Allan Chochinov use several analogies to describe life before and after marriage. Here's one that happens too often: Before marriage, that person was charming and noble, after marriage, CHERNOBYL! Sadly, many are unwilling to work at making their marriage better each year.

Jane and I have found that life is better now than before we were married. We have gone from knowing very little about each other to loving each other deeply. Where we were once struggling and competing, we now have peace and contentment. Our physical intimacy has grown to the point where it enhances our unity with love and tenderness. Our marriage just keeps getting better because we work at it.

Marriage is what you make it and what you believe it can be! Believe in yours!

Marriage Moments:

- What are some phrases you would use to describe your marriage "before and after"?

- Who are your mentors in marriage growth?

Pray Together

Don't Get Cocky!

Job 5:2-3

"Resentment kills a fool, and envy slaves the simple.
I myself have seen a fool taking root, but
suddenly his house was cursed."

If your marriage is full of contentment . . . if it seems the choices you've made are finally proving to be worthy . . . if life is better than you ever thought it could be, consider the source of your blessing — Jesus Christ. Without His hand at work in our lives, all of our plans and decisions and promises are for nothing.

The American way of life is to push ourselves to the top of the heap, then sit back and admire what we have accomplished. But the Christian recognizes that only a fool brings praise to his own life and disregards the blessings that come from God.

Today is a good day to thank the Lord for His blessings in your life and His special benediction on your marriage.

Marriage Moments:

• Do you express your thanks to God for the blessings He has given?

• List five blessings you see in your marriage.

Pray Together

Who's Conducting This Show?

Proverbs 16:9

"In his heart a man plans his course, but the Lord determines his steps."

Marilyn shared this vision the Lord gave her as she listened to God during her devotions. She found herself before a large orchestra with the conductor's baton in her hand. Feeling very out of place, she attempted to begin conducting. But when she signaled for the musicians to begin, the sound was atrocious.

Out of the corner of her eye she saw someone walking toward her. She realized it was Jesus Christ. He took the baton and pointed her to a vacant chair in the orchestra pit. Then, with precision, He lifted the baton and signaled the orchestra to begin. Suddenly a beautiful melody filled the room as the talented musicians followed the Master Conductor.

Is God the conductor of your marriage? Let Him lead and discover the harmony and unity He can bring.

Marriage Moments:

• In what areas have you sought to conduct your own lives?

• How can you trust these areas to Christ? Will you?

Pray Together

14

Confidential

Psalms 40:4

"Blessed is the man who makes the Lord his trust."

There are certain things husbands and wives should only share with each other. Whether they are intimate physical issues, needs of the children or personal problems that arise, these things need to be kept private. No matter what . . . they're confidential.

This confidentiality builds trust and oneness in the marriage relationship that is essential for its survival. In a healthy marriage, the partners have no need to share personal details with others. Such lack of respect only brings hurt and humiliation.

Marriage Moments:

- Do you keep private matters private?

- What issues will you agree to only share with each other?

Pray Together

The Cover Story

Jeremiah 31:3

"The Lord appeared to us in the past, saying:
'I have loved you with an everlasting love; I have
drawn you with loving-kindness.'"

After our fourth child, Anna Elizabeth, was born, my wife turned to me one day as we sat on the couch and said, "You can't help it, it's just there." "What's there?" I asked. "Love," she replied. She was right. Anna hadn't done or said anything to make us love her, but the love was there. God gave us that "built-in" love.

Sometimes in marriage we have an initial "love," but hurts and pain cause us to begin to cover-up our feelings. Soon the pile of frustration is so large we can't see the underlying love. The only way to remove the pile is through God's gifts of forgiveness, honesty and grace.

Marriage Moments:

• Have you "covered-up" love for your mate?

• What causes you to do this? What are some practical ways you can remove the frustrations in your marriage?

Pray Together

16

I Didn't See That

Isaiah 5:21

"Woe to those who are wise in their own eyes and
clever in their own sight."

One of the benefits of marriage that I've experienced is a new
awareness of my own inconsistencies and weaknesses. My wife has
been very helpful in pointing them out! Sincerely, she has been patient
in allowing me to grow in these areas.

The key to my growth has been an acceptance of her evaluations.
Sometimes they have been frustrating to hear, but as I have continued
to sort through all the comments, they have been accurate. With her
loving support and God's grace, I am changing and growing every day.
I'm grateful for her faithfulness to me.

Marriage Moments:

- What has your spouse pinpointed in your life that required you to
  rise to a higher level of relational and/or spiritual growth?

- How do you receive constructive criticism from your marriage
  partner?

Pray Together

Do-It-Yourself Kit

Ephesians 5:31

"For this reason a man will leave his father and mother and be united to his wife, and the two will become one flesh."

I like do-it-yourself kits. I enjoy taking an unfinished product and forming it into a beautifully crafted piece of work. How rewarding it is to be involved in its formation and perfection!

Marriage is like a do-it-yourself kit. It includes: two people, some disassembled parts, God's book of instruction (the Bible) and glue (Jesus Christ). The finished product will require years of hard work and dedication. But what a reward there is for those stick with it and patiently follow the instructions!

Marriage Moments:

- As marriage partners, are both of you giving your best to the marriage building process? What could each of you do better?

- Where do you see Christ bringing you unity on a daily basis?

Pray Together

18

We Are Driven

Psalm 62:1

"My soul finds rest in God alone."

"We are driven." This short advertising slogan used by a national car company is effective because it represents our western philosophy of life. We are driven to succeed. Jobs, possessions, goals and desires propel us onward, ever searching for success.

Have you ever gone away for a vacation, only to come home feeling guilty for doing nothing? Sure! We all have. We are so driven we think we can't relax.

It is necessary for couples to schedule periods of rest and relaxation together. They can be times of renewal and refreshment for both the body and the spirit.

Marriage Moments

- What drives you?
  - Getting things done - L
  - Success - P
  - Help people
  - make a difference
- Are you resting and refocusing together? (Plan a time . . . NOW!)

Feb 6th

Pray Together

A Little Elbow Room

Genesis 1:27

"So God created man in his own image, in the image of God he created him; male and female he created them."

At times, marriage can feel cramped. Husbands and wives often fail to give each other the freedom they need to be themselves and grow and develop at their own pace.

It is all too easy for me to expect my spouse to conform to my way of thinking, to act like I do and have the same desires I have. But this is not God's plan for marriage.

Only when spouses learn to let go and let each other be uniquely themselves in Christ will their marriages begin to grow. Cramping each others' personalities and opinions results in barriers to marriage harmony.

Marriage Moments:

- Does your spouse give you enough "elbow room" in your marriage?

- Are you too opinionated and domineering to allow freedom for growth in areas of weakness in your marriage? What are those areas?

Pray Together

20

I Think I Can

2 Timothy 2:13

"If we are faithless, he will remain faithful, for he cannot disown himself."

Remember the story of the little engine that said, "I think I can, I think I can"? What happened at the end? He accomplished what it was that he was trying to do all along. I like to think that I am like that engine — persistent, willing and driven.

But even if I cannot, God can. He is forever faithful . . . forever true . . . forever God. Even if I think I can . . . I KNOW HE CAN. He can bless our marriage. He can bring healing to our wounds. He can guide us into a holy relationship. What will you let Him do for you?

Marriage Moments:

- What do you believe Christ can do in your marriage?

- Are you being faithful to Him in every area of your life? Where can you improve?

Pray Together

Invisible Fencing

Psalm 91:9-10

"If you make the Most High your dwelling — even the Lord, who is my refuge — then no harm will befall you, no disaster will come near your tent."

Are you familiar with those invisible fences that surround your property and keep your pets from straying? If they try to cross the boundary, an electric shock prompts them to stay back. It only takes a few shocks to train them to stay in the yard.

Marriages need invisible fences. Boundaries provide protection from extramarital affairs and other harmful patterns of behavior. Here are several potential "invisible fences" for your marriage.

1. An accountability partner.
2. Daily study of God's Word.
3. Open, honest communication with your spouse.
4. A child's prodding questions.

Be careful if you think you're beyond the danger zone. Take heed, lest you fall.

Marriage Moments:

- What invisible fences of protection have you been using to guard your marriage?

- Are you doing anything risky near or outside those barriers?

Pray Together

Seeing Through the Fog

1 Corinthians 13:12

"Now we see but a poor reflection as in a mirror;
then we shall see face to face."

The U. S. Bureau of Standards recently released statistics related to its study of fog. The goal was to determine how much water existed in a dense fog covering seven city blocks and extending one hundred feet high. Amazingly, when this large area of fog was condensed into water, it filled one eight-ounce glass.

Just as the dense fog described above can shut down an international airport, Satan has a way of turning small problems into massive conflicts which shut down communication in marriage. But when Satan's fog is condensed, it is easy to see that the problems can be worked out and overcome.

Don't let an eight-ounce problem become the fog that overtakes your marriage and robs it of its joy. Ask the Son to come along beside you and burn off the fog that you may clearly see the road ahead.

Marriage Moments:

- Are you aware of any minor problems that have grown into major conflicts? Are you honest about your involvement in causing these conflicts?

- Where could you go for counseling if the fog continues to build? Do you need to take that step today?

Pray Together

I'm Following You

1 Peter 4:10

"Each one should use whatever gift he has received
to serve others, faithfully administering God's
grace in its various forms."

An edgy, irritable mother showed her frustration in the grocery store parking lot. Her son, being a normal child, wanted to help push the cart. Finally he was allowed to, and as he trailed along behind her, he said, "Mom, I'm following you." Her cold and unfriendly response came back, "Yea, I know. You're like a disease."

Does your spouse ever get on your nerves? Do you sometimes wish he would just leave you alone? Is her presence a bother at times — like a disease? Don't forget that your marriage is a gift from God — one that is worthy of your highest service. Serving each other with joy and love is the only way to turn this disease into a blessing.

Marriage Moments:
- When does your spouse get on your nerves?

- If you consider legitimate interruptions a bother, ask your accountability partner to question you about your progress in this area weekly. Who will you tell to hold you accountable?

Pray Together

24

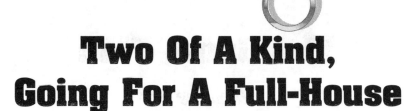

Two Of A Kind, Going For A Full-House

Psalm 127:3

"Sons are a heritage from the Lord, children a reward from him."

Most couples look forward to the time when they will have children. Sadly, some couples are unable to procreate — a situation which puts great stress on the marriage relationship. It is difficult to see God's hand at work in the midst of such times.

If you have been blessed with children, think for a moment of the pain of those who have not. Pray for them. If you are one of those couples that are struggling with this burden, be assured that God can fulfill your heart's desires in ways you cannot imagine. Trust Him to do it!

Marriage Moments:

- Who do you know who has struggled with childlessness and could use your words of encouragement?

- In what way will you allow God to work in your marriage to bring about healing for your pain?

Pray Together

The Game Plan

Ecclesiastes 4:8

"For whom am I toiling . . . and why am I depriving myself of enjoyment?"

Do you know couples who seem to have no fun in their marriage? How about you? Do you play games together? Do you laugh with each other and enjoy the time spent in fun? Most couples have fun in their dating relationship but discontinue those times of enjoyment soon after the wedding.

Make it your goal to find ways to put the fun back in your marriage. Enjoy a sporting event, take a bike ride, go on a picnic, invite some friends over for a game of Monopoly — whatever it takes, do it! You must make the effort if it is going to happen.

Marriage Moments:

- What do you do to have fun?

- Establish a "game plan" for times of enjoyment together.

Pray Together

The Girl Is Mine

Song of Songs 1:2

"Let him kiss me with the kisses of his mouth —
for your love is more delightful than wine."

I enjoy giving my wife a little PDA (Public Display of Affection). An occasional peck on the lips, holding hands at the mall, playing footsie at the restaurant, and walking with our arms around each other are ways we communicate our love without speaking.

Why is this important? There are several reasons. First, it's a statement to her that I love her and want to show her my love. Second, it's a statement to others who may attempt to challenge the security of our relationship. Third, it sets a great example for our children and others we may meet. Fourth, it's fun!

Start looking for ways that you can openly show your love. A little PDA can make a difference!

Marriage Moments:

- Do other people see you caring for each other? How? If not, why not?

- It's important to agree on the methods of PDA you will use. What methods can we agree on? Holding hands? Opening the door? Walking arm in arm?

Pray Together

Goalden Moments

Psalm 48:14

"For this God is our God for ever and ever; he will be
our guide even to the end."

Twice a year Jane and I go away together. Part of our time away is spent defining specific goals for our marriage and our children. We don't etch them in stone or create monstrous tasks, but rather we agree together that certain specifics ought to occur over the following months. More than anything, it's a time to discuss our future and ask the Lord to bless our efforts.

Every marriage needs goals, for goals bring focus and unity to marriage. They allow partners to agree on a course of action for the future and point the relationship in the right direction. Goals help strengthen purpose and solidify priorities. And those who seek God's will for the future will surely know His blessing and guiding hand.

Marriage Moments:

- What goals have you established for your marriage? If none, agree on three together.

- Have you sought to keep Christ in your decision making process? How?

Pray Together

Cooking Your Own Goose

Proverbs 16:32

"Better a patient man than a warrior, a man who controls his temper than one who takes a city."

Those who possess a boiling temper most often allow it to spill over on the ones they love — husband, wife and children. Most of us would agree that much pain is endured by those who experience the anger of their spouses. Ironically, my boiling temper cooks my own goose. Although damage is inflicted on my partner, a deeper problem is exposed — my inability to control my own behavior.

Have you lost your temper at home this week? Have you asked the Lord to teach you how to control your temper? Christ can help us with temper control, but we must be obedient to Him and willing to examine ourselves honestly in the light of the standard He sets for us.

Marriage Moments:

- In your marriage, how often does your temper flare and what are the usual results?

- What could you do to keep yourself from reaching these boiling points? Who will hold you accountable?

Pray Together

That's Not Green Grass, It's Artificial Turf

1 Corinthians 10:13

"No temptation has seized you except what is common to man. And God is faithful; he will not let you be tempted beyond what you can bear. But when you are tempted, he will also provide a way out so that you can stand up under it."

Before sensing and following God's call into the ministry, I served as the Financial Director of a hospital. My wife and I had been married for several years. The newness of our marriage had worn off, and we were experiencing a period of marital conflict. One evening as I worked late, a young lady came into my office and propositioned me. I was faced with the biggest temptation of my life. Because of the frustrations in my marriage, the grass looked green on her side of the fence.

God helped me see that the "green grass" was really "artificial turf." Giving in to what I thought looked good would have been disastrous for my own marriage. How grateful I am that He kept me from making that mistake!

Marriage Moments:

- Are either of you in any way jeopardizing the moral integrity of your marriage?

- What can you do to build more safeguards around your marriage?

Pray Together

30

The Green, Green Grass of Home

Galatians 5:16

"Live by the Spirit, and you will not gratify the desires of the sinful nature."

Mowing the grass is not my favorite chore, but I do it faithfully because I enjoy having a beautiful lawn. I like the wide open spaces the best — there are no trees or rocks or flower beds to slow me down. Many times I've cut those easy stretches first, only to glance over and see the trim work yet to be done.

Marriage is a lot like mowing the lawn. All too often, we work on the easy stretches, avoiding those areas that take more time and require closer attention. The result? Overgrown patches that cause our marriages to lose their beauty. Take time today to begin working on some of these areas and start to recapture the joy you once knew as husband and wife.

Marriage Moments:

- What are some areas of marriage you enjoy working at together? What areas do you dislike "trimming" or discussing?

- Share some ideas on how to eliminate these obstacles in your relationship.

Pray Together

Hall of Fame

Galatians 3:9

"So those who have faith are blessed along
with Abraham, the man of faith."

Paul Harvey, the news commentator, often highlights couples who have been faithfully married for many years. It's not uncommon for him to claim that a certain couple has known fifty, sixty, and even seventy years of wedded bliss.

It seems the frequency of meeting these long-term partners is diminishing. With the escalation of the divorce rate in our country, we may someday discover it's easier to find a person who's been married thirty times rather than thirty years.

Think of the couples you know who have been married for many years and have exhibited Christ-like love to each other. Put them in your mental "hall of fame" and let their marriages be a model for your lifelong partnership.

Marriage Moments:

- Get in touch with one of the couples you know who have been married many years. Thank them for their godly example.

- Are you living with joy and anticipation of the many years of marriage that lie ahead for you? Why or why not?

Pray Together

Keep Your Head Up

Proverbs 4:25

"Let your eyes look straight ahead, fix your gaze
directly before you."

As a boy, I often watched my grandfather's cows graze in the open pasture. In the morning, they would be by the barn enjoying the food and water he had provided. As they began to graze with their heads down, they slowly meandered this way and that without any obvious direction. Soon they would look up with a bit of surprise as if to say, "Hey . . . how'd I get here?" Without knowing it, they had nibbled their way a good distance from the barn.

Marriages suffer when husbands and wives fail to keep their heads up and their eyes focused on what is ahead. Discouragement, jealousy, pride and indifference are the things which continue to pull us downward, away from what is really important. Balance will come only when we lift up our heads and fasten our eyes on the Savior.

Marriage Moments:

• What causes you to "put your head down"?

• How can you encourage your spouse to "be alert" and "keep focus" in your relationship?

Pray Together

I Can Hear It

1 John 3:18

"Dear children, let us not love with words or tongue
but with actions and in truth."

John Francis, an elderly gentleman in our church, once shared his greatest experience as a grandfather. His little granddaughter recently came to him and said, "Grandpa, I know you love me." Not expecting this comment, John was a bit surprised and countered, "Well, tell me how you know." She replied, "I can hear it with my heart."

What a beautiful picture. It is easy to tell each other, "I love you." But the real test of love lies in our actions. Can your spouse honestly say, "I know you love me — I can hear it with my heart"?

Marriage Moments:

• Describe your spouse's love for you. What does your heart feel?

• How are you seeking to love your mate as Christ loved the church?

Pray Together

He Delivers For You

Deuteronomy 20:4

"For the Lord your God is the one who goes with you to fight for you against your enemies to give you victory."

I recently watched a couple go through very difficult circumstances brought on by the husband's co-workers. During this time of crisis, the couple found their strength in Christ and in each other. I recall how the husband shared with me the way Christ used certain people in his life to lead him in the divine way.

Often difficult circumstances will bring disharmony between married people. This is not God's design. Every experience can become a stepping stone instead of a stumbling block, if we so choose. God can use struggles, pain, hurt — and even difficult people — to bring us closer to Him. Seek His wisdom today and let Him show you the way to go.

Marriage Moments:
- When you face problems, do you grow closer together or farther apart? Why?

- Do you turn to God first with your difficulties?

Pray Together

Hold Up Your Corner

1 Corinthians 7:24

"Each man, as responsible to God, should remain in the
situation God called him to."

Envision, if you will, a large breakable object that requires two people to carry it. If either person lets go, that delicate item will fall to the ground and shatter into a million pieces.

Now picture marriage as the breakable object. The two carriers are you and your spouse. Once you said, "I do," you became responsible for all the commitments and promises stated in your wedding vows. If either you or your partner fails to live up to these responsibilities, the marriage will break apart. Make sure you continue to hold up your corner, that this beautiful thing called your marriage may stay intact.

Marriage Moments:

- Are you holding up your corner in this marriage? Does your spouse feel you are?

- What could you do to enhance the "holding up" process?

Pray Together

36

Honesty Is The Best Policy

Proverbs 11:1

"The Lord abhors dishonest scales, but accurate weights are his delight."

Quite often in marriage counseling I request to meet individually with each partner. It is amazing what I hear in these meetings. Without fail, the majority of these husbands and wives bring issues to me they keep secret from each other.

I understand why we often feel this way, but true communication in marriage will never occur without complete openness and honesty between spouses. Total honesty can be both frightening and intimidating, but its rewards are tremendous. I know from experience, for it took my wife and me eight years to begin opening ourselves to each other. But because we did, what a long way we have come! And what a solid foundation we have for our life together!

Marriage Moments:

- Are there areas in your marriage you would love to discuss but fear addressing?

- What steps can you take to become more open and honest?

Pray Together

"Honey-Do" List

Habakkuk 3:18

"I will rejoice in the Lord, I will be joyful in God my Savior."

I'm sure you've heard of a "Honey-Do" list. It's a list of tasks to do around the house, created by one spouse for the other. However, there's just something about someone else telling us what to do that causes us to put it off until the last minute. By then, it is often too late. Even though the task is accomplished, it has become a point of contention and stress.

Consider the joy it might give your spouse and the corresponding unity you might experience if you work together at accomplishing the tasks on the list. Show each other that you're willing to put forth the effort needed to bring harmony to your marriage. Work as a team; you're trying to win, not play one-on-one.

Marriage Moments:

- What tasks are on your current "honey-do" list?

- How are you accomplishing these tasks together? What can each of you do to make the work more enjoyable?

Pray Together

38

A House Of Love

Psalm 127:1b

"Unless the Lord watches over the city, the watchmen
stand guard in vain."

Each home has a reputation connected to it. If you had to identify a
nickname synonymous with your home, which words would you choose?

_____ Loving	_____ Frustrating	_____ Safe
_____ Joyful	_____ Pliable	_____ Threatening
_____ Blended	_____ Forgiving	_____ United
_____ Exciting	_____ Welcoming	_____ Fearful
_____ Uncertain	_____ Confusing	_____ Peaceful

Which words would your children choose? The neighbors? Your
friends?

Now, circle the words that you want to represent your home. Ask
the Lord for wisdom to build your home with these defining words as
a foundation.

Marriage Moments:

- How do you influence your home? Are your contributions more
  positive or negative?

- What can you begin to do now to alleviate some of the negative
  words attached to your home?

Pray Together

Howdy Duty!

Galatians 6:8

"The one who sows to please his sinful nature, from that nature will reap destruction; the one who sows to please the Spirit, from the Spirit will reap eternal life."

Many people wonder why they have to carry out certain responsibilities in the marriage relationship. Why must we continue to work out our differences? Why must we battle to keep the barriers down? Why must we be faithful to each other? Why? Why? Why? The answer is very simple. Our goal in life is to fear God and fulfill the duties He has assigned to us. He has placed us in this place for this time and it is here we are to faithfully obey Him.

The consequences of our actions are detailed in today's verse. Those who faithfully carry out their duties and responsibilities will reap the rewards of heaven. Those who choose to dishonor God and please themselves will know a different kind of reward. What will you choose to do?

Marriage Moments:

- What are some things you don't like to do but you know they are your duty?

- List several specific blessings you have received as a direct result of being faithful to God in your marriage relationship.

Pray Together

No Huddle Offense

Proverbs 4:2

"I will give you sound learning, so do not forsake my teaching."

I recently watched the Denver Broncos' offensive team take possession of the football and execute several plays in a row without huddling. The quarterback, John Elway, skillfully guided the rest of the team through a series of plays without calling each one in advance. It was obvious the team had prepared for this event. Each player knew exactly what to do. The smoothness of their execution was a result of many hours of practice and discipline.

When situations arise in marriage, how do you react? If you have spent time together in God's Word; if you have communicated to each other your hopes and fears; if you have decided upon a game plan — then your reaction should be spontaneous. Like the Broncos, you will know exactly what to do.

Marriage Moments:

- When you face situations that require you to go on the offensive, how do you react as a team?

- Knowing the importance of a huddle, take time to plan together now for upcoming situations.

Pray Together

A Piece Of Humble Pie

Proverbs 11:2

"When pride comes, then comes disgrace,
but with humility comes wisdom."

Humility is one of the hardest virtues to attain. Our culture promotes a "me first" attitude. I can be the best and have the most, and who cares about anyone else? But God's way is one of humbleness and self-sacrifice. Consider the example He gave us — Jesus Christ. His humility led Him to die on the cross — a death that brought us eternal life.

We must seek to follow Christ's example — especially in marriage — for practicing humility brings wisdom and understanding to the relationship. Too many marriages fail because partners refuse to get rid of the "I am better than you" attitude. The death of pride can bring about new life in the Spirit and new beginnings in marriage.

Marriage Moments:

- Are you humble? (Let your spouse give some input.)

- What could you do to be more humble in your relationship?

Pray Together

Hurry Up
And Slow Down

Psalm 62:1a

"My soul finds rest in God alone."

Why do we rush so? Why do we go through life in a panic without taking time to enjoy every moment? So much time is spent planning for the future that we fail to see what is good today.

Marriages can flounder when partners neglect to give attention to each day's needs and accomplishments. When husbands and wives don't enjoy the present together, why look forward to the future?

My advice is this: Stop wishing for what was and dreaming about what could be. Put your efforts into making each day the best day of your marriage. Your memories will become much sweeter and your future much brighter.

Marriage Moments:

• What kind of pace are you setting as a couple?

• Are you enjoying the daily routines of marriage life, or are you looking too much to the future? What happened today that you enjoyed?

Pray Together

If I Were In Charge

Proverbs 3:5-6

"Trust in the Lord with all your heart and lean not on your own understanding; in all your ways acknowledge him, and he will make your paths straight."

My son's third grade class was given this assignment: Write an article about what you would do if you were in charge of the world.
He wrote:

> If I were in charge of the world I would cancel Barney and Power Rangers. I would change everyone's skin to the same color so people would get along and then I would keep girls from always getting in the way. I would also add being able to drive when you were five years old.

As I read his ideas and those of his classmates, I thought how wonderful it is to know God's in charge. It's not up to us to figure out how to bring order to the universe. We can put our trust in Him today, for He understands it all.

Marriage Moments:

• If you were in charge of all marriages, what would you do?

• Are you practicing these principles in your own marriage?

Pray Together

Follow The Instructions

Psalm 32:8

"I will instruct you and teach you in the way you should go; I will counsel you and watch over you."

Have you ever tried to put something together without following the instructions? If so, then you know that the end result is usually not what you wanted it to be.

The Bible is our instruction book for life. In it is all the wisdom we need. Jane and I have never faced a question in our marriage that could not be answered by God's Word. If we are patient and diligent in our search for answers, God is always faithful to show us, through His Word, the path to take.

When struggles and questions come your way, turn to the Bible first. Use other resources only to affirm what it says. If you follow the instructions, the finished product will be put together correctly.

Marriage Moments:

• What issue are you currently facing that needs God's instruction?

• Where do you usually turn first when you deal with tough issues? Others? God? Self?

Pray Together

I Promise

Psalm 119:50

"Your promise preserves my life."

History will record "Promise Keepers," founded by Bill McCartney, as a great movement of Christianity. The movement calls upon Christian men to take a stand in their homes, their communities and their jobs. It challenges them to remain faithful to their marriage vows and be examples of love and leadership to their families.

Keeping promises is more than a verbal phrase; it's daily action. I want my children to see that I love my wife, my family and my God. I intend to show that love each day in my words and actions. My prayer is that my children will follow my example and will grow up to be promise keepers, too.

Marriage Moments:

- You promised "till death do us part." How are you doing?

- How could you be a better keeper of your promises?

Pray Together

"I Still Do"

Colossians 3:18-19

"Wives, submit to your husband, as is fitting in the Lord.
Husbands, love your wives and do not be harsh with them."

One of the joys of my profession is the opportunity to conduct marriage retreats. At each closing session, I ask couples to face each other and repeat the vows they said years before. But this time, instead of saying "I do," I ask them to say "I still do." "I still promise . . . before God . . . to love and to honor . . . for better, for worse . . . till death do us part."

Too often, wedding vows are left at the altar with the presiding minister. We need to daily remind each other — and ourselves — of the promises we made. Change "I do" to "I still do" and let your spouse know of your continued love and dedication.

Marriage Moments:

- Have you told your husband or wife "I still do" lately?

- Laugh and cry together as you recall memories from your wedding day.

Pray Together

Here Comes The Judge

Matthew 7:1

"Do not judge, or you too will be judged."

It is always easier to see someone else's faults than look at our own. Nowhere is this more true than in the marriage relationship. Husbands and wives are all too quick to point out the other's shortcomings. And the more they focus on the negative, the quicker the marriage is on the rocks.

To be honest, we each have a bit of housecleaning to be done. No one is exempt from failures and weaknesses. One of the reasons we find fault in others is because it's too difficult to face our own. Scripture teaches us to look at and deal with our own imperfections and let God be the judge of all. We must not waste our time judging others, for surely we would not want others to judge us.

Marriage Moments:

- Do you judge your spouse? How often and about what issues?

- How can you focus on your own shortcomings rather than your spouse's? How can you work as a team to overcome them and grow together?

Pray Together

48

This Is Killing Me

Galatians 2:20a

"I have been crucified with Christ and I no longer live,
but Christ lives in me."

Recently, I came home from work with a negative attitude. Though I didn't speak any unkind or hurtful words, my facial expression and body language obviously replaced my tongue and brought a negative spirit into the home. Later, as I asked the Lord for wisdom to deal with the frustration of my day, He prompted me to apologize to my wife for my inner thoughts which had caused this discontent.

I carefully approached her and apologized for having critical thoughts toward her. She was disheartened. Her specific comment was, "Just knowing you had those critical thoughts toward me is very painful." I realized my unspoken words hurt her as deeply as brutal outspoken language would have. In order to eliminate these thoughts from entering my mind, I must begin to imitate Christ. How? By continuing to die to myself and my desires and focusing only on Christ. It hurts, but it heals.

Marriage Moments:

- How have you "died to self" in your relationship?

- Pray specifically for guidance from the Lord in this process of giving yourself completely to Him.

Pray Together

Just Leave Me Alone

Leviticus 19:11c

"Do not deceive one another."

It's funny how married couples communicate. We rarely say exactly what we mean — especially in the heat of an argument. It took me a few years to figure out that when my wife says, "Leave me alone," what she really means is, "Dan, please change your behavior and attitude and hold me."

I have my phrases, too. In a heated moment a silly phrase like, "Why did you marry me in the first place?" means "Please tell me you love me and think I'm great." "Just forget it" should be translated "I want to be honest and talk more." Our words can be so deceiving.

That's one of the reasons it is so difficult to understand each other. Think of how different it would be if we spoke our true thoughts — tempered by God's love. Deceitfulness can be a terrible thing, but the truth can bring healing and wholeness.

Marriage Moments:

- Share with your spouse the real meanings behind your favorite phrases.

- Create some new phrases to use as encouragement for each other.

Pray Together

Listening Together

Proverbs 1:5a

"Let the wise listen and add to their learning."

When Jane and I are faced with decisions, we make it our top priority to listen to God for specific direction. His guidance has been obvious throughout our life together. How do we do this? First we go to a quiet place and, after praying together, we stop and quietly listen to His voice.

A dear, elderly lady named Mary Geegh shared with me this simple yet profound way of discerning God's will. In her life as a missionary, she experienced incredible answers to prayer by just stopping and listening to God. It has been a joy for us to experience together this method of communication with Him.

Marriage Moments:

- How often do you quiet yourselves before the Lord to listen to His direction?

- What areas of your marriage would be enhanced if you took time to listen to God? List three specific areas that need His guidance.

Pray Together

It's Bigger Than It Looks

Isaiah 2:3

". . . He will teach us his ways, so that we may
walk in his paths . . ."

Edwin Peterson, an elderly man, shared with me how, as a five-year-old boy, he was working with his grandfather in the work shed. Edwin reached out to touch a shiny saw his grandfather was using and his grandfather said, "Don't touch that, it's bigger than it looks." Edwin told how that phrase stuck with him through tempting situations as a young boy. It helped him make wise decisions through his teen years and even into marriage.

Wisdom in marriage includes walking in God's paths and staying away from situations that are bigger than they look.

Marriage Moments:

- Are you — individually or as a couple — entering any situations that may be bigger than they look? Are you seeking God for specific direction in these decisions?

- What paths of spiritual growth are you experiencing together?

Pray Together

52

Look Before You Leap

Job 11:18

"You will be secure, because there is hope; you will look about you and take your rest in safety."

My boyhood friend, Robert, and I usually tried to sneak a swim on warm summer days at our neighbor's pond in the quaint little town of Six Mile, South Carolina. We would strip down to our underwear and jump with delight into the deepest part of the water.

On one occasion, as we were swimming toward the shore, a snake wiggled out of the bushes and started to swim toward us. Needless to say, we set a swimming pace that would have won the Olympics.

Sometimes we leap into the pond of marriage without first "checking the water." We will be better prepared for marriage and the decisions that follow if we look to Christ before we leap. He will help us determine any dangers or trouble spots ahead.

Marriage Moments:

- What "ponds" are you considering jumping into? How have you sought His direction for this endeavor?

- What "checks and balances" can you establish to protect you from jumping in without His guidance?

Pray Together

Look Over Here

Proverbs 8:27

"I was there when he set the heavens in place, when he marked out the horizon on the face of the deep."

Do you ever do something to get your spouse's attention? I do. Sometimes I get silly and show off my muscles or impress her with my sexy smile. Sometimes I get all dressed up and good-smelling and pour on the charm. My goal is to be so suave and debonair that she can't resist her desire to be close to me.

It's funny, isn't it — we love to know that who we are is attractive to that special person. We want to be assured that we are important to them. Our Bible verse today reminds us that the very fact that we were created by God makes us special and unique. If we continue to grow in Christ, our attraction to each other will remain strong and healthy.

Marriage Moments:

- Look at your spouse today and invite him or her over to your turf. Put on your best smile or your most impressive pose. Be silly for a change.

- Renew your commitment to stand beside each other as you reflect the image of God.

Pray Together

54

Look Out And Look Up

Matthew 6:34a

"Do not worry about tomorrow,
for tomorrow will worry about itself."

Our future is unsure. We may set goals and follow plans to achieve those goals, but life has a way of forcing us to detour the secure pathways we've established.

God teaches us to always look up — not always the simplest thing to do, especially in the midst of trouble. Looking up comes more easily when we're on our knees. The humility and self-surrender of bowing before the Lord is a calm reminder of his lordship and our humanity. Together, through prayer, the God who owns our future will give us peace and assurance to face tomorrow and all the tomorrows to come.

Marriage Moments:

• What uncertainties loom in your future?

• How often are you bringing these uncertainties to the Lord? Are you trusting Him with the outcome?

Pray Together

"I Love Jesus . . . Yes I Do"

Proverbs 8:17

"I love those who love me, and those who seek me find me."

At a large rally, people on one side of the audience began the chant, "We love Jesus, yes we do. We love Jesus, how 'bout you?" The other side of the audience echoed back, "We love Jesus, yes we do. We love Jesus, how 'bout you?"

Our homes also should be places of praise. Singing should echo from the walls, and rejoicing should fill the air. There should be no doubt that this is a place where "We love Jesus, yes we do!"

Marriage Moments:

• Does verbal praise echo back and forth in your home?

• How can you make your home a house of praise?
  List three ideas.

Pray Together

56

A Love Note

Proverbs 22:11

"He who loves a pure heart and whose speech is
gracious will have the king for his friend."

I was at the dinner table one evening, making conversation with
our children. We were recalling some funny incidents that had
occurred over the past few weeks when my wife abruptly stopped our
conversation and said, "Kids, you've got a great dad. Isn't it wonderful
how he makes us all laugh?" They all agreed, and we continued our
conversation, enjoying the laughter and the fun together.

It was just a simple little phrase, but it touched a special chord inside
my heart. I felt wanted, needed, useful, uniquely theirs and happy. I
was grateful to my wife for sending me that note of appreciation.

It's my turn to give my wife the same kind of love note. Exactly
when I'll say it, I'm not sure. I don't even know what words I'll use.
I just hope I can give her the same feeling that she gave me through her
words of appreciation.

Marriage Moments:

- When did you last interrupt a conversation to praise your mate?

- Are you content with the praise you receive from your marriage
  partner? How could you praise each other more?

Pray Together

You Look Maaavelous!

Song of Songs 1:15a

"How beautiful you are, my darling! Oh how beautiful!"

I've noticed a trend among divorced singles that annoys me. After the divorce, many men and women begin to physically discipline their bodies into shape and become much more concerned about their personal appearance. Obviously, part of the reason is to appear more attractive for a potential new relationship.

If people would do their best, look their best and be their best while they are still married, maybe there wouldn't be so many divorces. Taking care of myself says that I respect the body God has given me. It also says "I care" to my wife. When my wife says, "Thanks for taking care of yourself," I am inspired all the more to aggressively continue improving myself for her.

Marriage Moments:

- What physical discipline do you practice individually and together?

- Do you attempt to look your best for your mate?

Pray Together

It's A Miracle

Psalm 146:5-6a

"Blessed is he whose help is the God of Jacob, whose hope is in the Lord his God, the Maker of heaven and earth."

We have a little shelf in our home that holds mementos which remind us of some of the blessings God has given to us during our marriage. There's a souvenir from a trip we were privileged to take, a Matchbox replica of a car God provided for us and several other such keepsakes. They are constant reminders of Christ's involvement in our life together. We often visit our miracle shelf — especially during times of struggle — to recall once again that God loves us and is working in our lives.

Isn't it wonderful that God cares about our every need? He can bring about a miracle when it seems that all hope is gone. Take time today to be reminded of His blessings.

Marriage Moments:

• What blessings have you received from God during your marriage?

• How do you remind yourselves of those blessings?

Pray Together

A Profound Mystery

Ephesians 5:31-32a

"For this reason a man will leave his father and mother
and be united to his wife, and the two will become
one flesh. This is a profound mystery."

The mystery of two becoming one flesh can be illustrated with an artist's colors. If blue and red paint are mixed together, a new distinctive color is produced — purple.

When a man and a woman become husband and wife, they are united spiritually, emotionally, and physically by Almighty God. Scripture refers to this process as a profound mystery. The two are now one. This unity is not to be taken lightly, since it is a union ordained by our Maker. Our love for each other must be as pure and holy as His love for us.

Marriage Moments:
- Have you effectively left father and mother and created a union with each other? (Allow each other to share openly.)

- What are some specific ways you have become united in Christ?

Pray Together

The Straight And Narrow

Matthew 7:14

"Small is the gate and narrow the road that leads
to life, and only a few find it."

The world will tell us that we should be driving a certain kind of car, wearing the latest style of clothing and living a particular lifestyle. But we must not get caught up in all that hype. The Bible says the most important thing we will ever do is prepare for eternity. Our marriages should be constantly evaluated to make sure this is the focus. We should also be looking for ways to continually spur each other on in spiritual preparation for the moment we stand before God.

How? Pray... say ... grow ... love ... learn ... give ... sacrifice. Remember, it's a straight and narrow way. In a society that teaches tolerance, diversity and open mindedness, don't become confused. There *is* morality ... there *is* a standard ... there *is* a bigger purpose, and we have found it in Christ.

Marriage Moments:

- Do you keep your marriage focused on the "straight and narrow" way?

- What aspects of your marriage are easily distracted from this most important focus?

Pray Together

The Neckbone's Connected To The Headbone

Ephesians 5:28

"Husbands ought to love their wives as their own bodies.
He who loves his wife loves himself."

Joseph Garlington, a pastor in Virginia, says if he is the head of the home then his wife is the neck. She helps turn his head the way it ought to go and works with him to give their life direction.

Marriage is a team effort. One cannot give direction unless the other is willing to turn and cooperate. Both partners need each other to be complete and to make the marriage function. How thankful we should be that God, in His wisdom, designed marriage this way! For in His plan, each has a job to do that perfectly complements the other. The best results can be accomplished only when both work together.

Marriage Moments:

- What will be the result of your marriage if you try to take charge of it yourself?

- What two things could you do better if you worked together?

Pray Together

62

You Drive Me Nuts

James 1:2-4

"Consider it pure joy, my brothers, whenever you face trials of many kinds, because you know that the testing of your faith develops perseverance. Perseverance must finish its work so that you may be mature and complete not lacking anything."

There are times when my wife drives me nuts. I don't know what it is — the stress of the day, the conversation we're having, the weather — but sometimes I just can't wait to go into another room and be away from her for a little while. The funny thing is — I think there are times when she feels the same way about me!

All married couples get that feeling once in awhile. It comes from being so close that we begin to notice each other's little imperfections. We need to learn how to lighten up a little, laugh more often and teach ourselves to overlook the small faults that drive us crazy. Most of the time they're not important enough to worry about, anyway. Plus, if I spend some time looking at my own faults, I'll hardly have time to worry about someone else's, right?

Marriage Moments:

• Name something about your spouse that "drives you nuts."

• Laugh together about your differences.

Pray Together

Objects In Mirror Are Closer Than They Appear

James 1:23-24

"Anyone who listens to the word but does not do what it says is like a man who looks at his face in a mirror and, after looking at himself, goes away and immediately forgets what he looks like."

Have you looked in the mirror lately? Do you like what you see? Oh, I'm not talking about physical characteristics. No, I'm thinking about those hidden issues behind your eyes that are bringing disharmony to your marriage.

You see, change begins with *me*. If my marriage lacks harmony, it's up to *me* to do something about it. I cannot point a finger at my spouse and say, "You have to change."

God is willing to show me those areas that need change, and He is ready to give the help I need to bring about real harmony in my marriage. Am I ready and willing to do my part?

Marriage Moments:

- How often do you look into the mirror of your own life?

- Is it easier for you to spot areas of need in your spouse or in yourself?

Pray Together

Open The Door

2 Timothy 2:15

"Do your best to present yourself to God as one approved,
a workman who does not need to be ashamed and who
correctly handles the word of truth."

There are times when I don't feel comfortable opening the door —
at a hotel when the face in the peephole is unknown — at home, around
midnight, when the banging continues. We've all experienced that
moment of hesitation.

Most of us have also experienced it in marriage. There is a fear of
opening up an issue that is uncomfortable or embarrassing. However,
addressing the issue usually reveals another part of the relationship that
has never been fully explored. Opening that door can be a wonderful
opportunity to free ourselves of the debris hidden on the other side. A
new feeling of cleansing and wholeness sets in. That's a lot to gain
from one simple step! Go ahead — turn the knob!

Marriage Moments:

- What doors have you opened in the past? How have they built
  your relationship?

- Consider opening a new door today.

Pray Together

Pass It On

Deuteronomy 11:19

"Teach them to your children, talking about them when
you sit at home and when you walk along the road,
when you lie down and when you get up."

I stood with my children by Grandma and Grandpa's grave. My
five-year-old wanted to know if we were going to dig them up. The
three-year-old asked if she could take some of the little rocks home.
My eight-year-old understood he would probably stand over my grave
like this one day.

The night before, we had laughed as each of the children put on
Grandpa's hat and tipped it to one side or the other. I wish Grandpa had
known his great-grandchildren. He would have been proud. They
would have loved him.

My wife and I are making memories now which we will leave with our
children someday. The example we set in our marriage will be imitated by
those little ones who follow us. It is our responsibility to pass on to our
children the great truths of God's Word and the good news of His love.

Marriage Moments:

- Who are the children you influence by your example? Think of
  family and friends.

- Are you satisfied with the example you are modeling for them?
  How could you improve?

Pray Together

Come On, Nobody's Perfect

John 13:15

"I have set you an example that you should do as
I have done for you."

It's easy for married couples to expect perfection from each other. And when that partner doesn't live up to that expectation, the trouble begins.

Remember, Christ was the only one who attained perfection on earth. We can take steps toward becoming more like Him, but we will still make mistakes. And we cannot expect a higher level of perfection from our partners than what we ourselves have attained. Let us instead work on perfecting our love toward each other, that we may leave behind these score cards of mistakes and go forward with joy and anticipation for what lies ahead.

Marriage Moments:

- In what areas do you place unreasonable expectations on your marriage partner?

- What can you do to keep your expectations in check?

Pray Together

Picture Perfect

James 1:25

"The man who looks intently into the perfect law that gives freedom, and continues to do this, not forgetting what he has heard, but doing it — he will be blessed in what he does."

Have you ever taken a close look at a pictorial directory? Every person is wearing a smile. Every family looks content and happy. Even couples who have great marital conflict call a truce long enough for a photographer to capture a fake pose of joy.

What if the photographs revealed the true feelings behind those happy faces? How much hopelessness would we see? How much despair? How much hatred?

God can make the inside match the smile on the outside. He can change whatever is in your heart that is keeping you from the joy He offers. He can turn you inside out — make you a new person — give you happiness you never thought possible. Will you let Him?

Marriage Moments:

- Look at a photograph taken of you since you've been married. Does it reflect your true feelings?

- If not, draw a face that reflects that feeling. What can you do to keep your face smiling?

Pray Together

68

Play Now, Play Later

Nehemiah 8:10

"The joy of the Lord is your strength."

Remember the electricity that was in the air when you were dating that special someone? The first kiss, walking in the moonlight, baring your souls to each other — all these things brought sparks of joy and excitement to the relationship. Do you still have that electricity in your marriage? Or have you — like most of us — lost sight of it in all the mundane, everyday routines of life?

To keep that spark alive, revisit some of those things that brought such joy in the beginning. Go to the spot of your first date. Look at some old photos. Go parking. Laugh over old memories.

Go ahead . . . try it again for the very first time.

Marriage Moments:

• How often do you play together by dating, reminiscing, etc.?

• How can you add spark to your relationship?

Pray Together

Polish And Buff

Ephesians 1:4

"For he chose us in him before the creation of the world to be holy and blameless in his sight."

Have you seen those commercials on television? An old, dull, weather-beaten car is shown in a junk pile. The car is extracted from the heap and given a fresh coat of polish and an extensive buffing. The dull exterior explodes with a brilliant, smooth, colorful shine.

Sometimes I have dull spots in my life that need to be polished and buffed. My wife and I are faithful to notice these spots in each other and pray for the Lord to make us holy and blameless in these areas. Prayer is the best non-abrasive way to get our own lives to explode with the brilliance of Jesus Christ.

Marriage Moments:

- What has been your dull area this week? Attitudes? Spiritual life? Encouraging spirit?

- Have you chosen to criticize or pray for your partner when you notice those areas that need polish?

Pray Together

70

Practice Makes Perfect

Philippians 4:9

"Whatever you have learned or received or heard from me, or seen in me — put it into practice."

Mom would sit beside me on the piano bench. That dreaded metronome kept a steady pace as she conducted me through another piece of John Thompson's music. I didn't like it. My friends were out shooting hoops while I was enduring the torture of practicing the piano. Now, all I can say is, "Thanks, Mom!" A quiet room and an old upright piano bring back many memories, and a few minutes of playing give me much contentment.

My marriage needs a metronome every now and then. A solid, steady reminder of the importance of being faithful in the little things helps keep me on the right track. If I keep practicing, I will reap the joys of a sound marriage and a lasting relationship.

Marriage Moments:

- What principles are you practicing that are developing your marriage?

- What do you need to practice? (Love, care, forgiveness, devotion, communication, trust, etc.)

Pray Together

Pray Before You Go

Proverbs 14:29

"A patient man has great understanding, but a
quick-tempered man displays folly."

Here's a scenario we've all experienced. You come home from a
tough day at work. Your mind is spinning with work-related issues and
your body is tense and high-strung. The first words you share with
your spouse reflect impatience and criticism. A gloomy cloud settles
over the home, and the tension continues until bedtime — sometimes
into the next day.

What should you do? Try this. Write these words on a piece of
paper: PRAY BEFORE YOU GO. Put this note by your light switch
at work or on the dashboard of your car. Before you leave the office or
as you're driving home, pray for the Lord to help you live as if this
were the last day you would have with your spouse. God can change
you and make each homecoming a joyous occasion. Are you willing to
try it?

Marriage Moments:

- Do you have a problem with patience? Who struggles most?

- Will you determine to pray about your attitude before you arrive
  home?

Pray Together

72

The Ultimate Intimacy

Colossians 4:2

"Devote yourselves to prayer, being watchful and thankful."

Prayer is the best kept secret of marital joy. I often share with men the importance of being the spiritual leader in the home. But many men feel uncomfortable praying with their wives because it is intimidating or embarrassing for them. This is one of Satan's tricks.

A man can have intimate relations with his wife and feel no embarrassment whatsoever, but he claims the thought of praying with her makes him self-conscious. Doesn't that sound a little backward?

Christian husbands and wives praying together should be the rule, not the exception. After all, if God is to work in the marriage and bless the relationship, then He needs to be invited into the home daily. Coming before the Lord as one is the single most important thing a couple can do together. It is the ultimate intimacy.

Marriage Moments:
- Do you pray daily together? If not, why not?

- To help guide you in your prayers, make a list of prayer needs and appropriate them to different days of the week.

Pray Together

Practice What You Preach

Proverbs 6:23b

"The corrections of discipline are the way to life."

I have a way of making negative comments to my wife at the most inappropriate moments. Comments like: "Why don't you work on improving that?" or "Have you prayed for a good attitude today?" or "You're losing it with the kids, Honey!" As soon as these insensitive words are out of my mouth, I feel ashamed. My wife needs loving encouragement, not constant criticism.

Instead of pointing my finger and itemizing her faults, I need to look in the mirror and take stock of my own shortcomings. Then I need to pray — for her needs, for my own insensitivity, for the life we share. In order to become more like Christ, I need to practice the love and kindness I preach about so often.

Marriage Moments:

- Allow your spouse to share with you some qualities you need to "practice" rather than "preach."

- Are you both willing to work to grow in these areas? How?

Pray Together

Our Future Is Predictable

Revelation 21:2

"I saw the Holy City, the new Jerusalem, coming down
out of heaven from God, prepared as a bride
beautifully dressed for her husband."

In the middle of an unpredictable society we need security and steadiness — something predictable. We do not know when we will die. We can only guess what life on earth will be like in the future. Our children's futures are uncertain.

However, in the middle of all the uncertainties, our future is absolutely predictable. We can know what lies ahead. Jesus said, "I am the way." His death on the cross assures us of the opportunity of being with Him when the new Jerusalem comes. My wife and I have decided to live for Christ on earth so we may live together in heaven for eternity. God has given us this promise. It's predictable.

Marriage Moments:

- Are you certain of your future? If not, pray for God's forgiveness and accept His salvation.

- Whom are you influencing for Christ?

Pray Together

A Quiet Cove

Psalm 25:20

"Guard my life and rescue me; let me not be put to shame, for I take refuge in you."

You've seen those quiet, little coves that are hidden away from the roaring surge of the main body of water. The waters are blue and calm. The trees sway in the breeze and the beach glitters in the sunlight. The serenity and peacefulness of such places beckon us, for here it seems we are closer to God.

Marriages need to have those quiet, peaceful moments. The seas of life can toss us to and fro, but a visit to a quiet cove offers serenity that renews strength and brings peace. Find your quiet coves together. Know when they are needed. Hide away as often as you can.

Marriage Moments:

- Where do you find serenity for your marriage?

- What can you do to create more "cove" moments with each other?

Pray Together

76

The Quicker Picker Upper

1 Thessalonians 4:18

"Therefore encourage each other with these words."

Remember the top brand paper towel that was faster than any others in cleaning up spills? It was called the "quicker-picker-upper." It was strong, absorbent and dependable.

That's the kind of husband I want to be — a "quicker-picker-upper." When my wife is tired and discouraged, I want to be there to pick her up with my words of encouragement and my deeds of love. It is not up to me to be her critic or her judge. It *is* my responsibility to be her friend and companion.

May the Lord help us to give freely of ourselves to our wives and our husbands, that they may be strengthened and encouraged each new day.

Marriage Moments:

• What phrases do you use to encourage and uplift your spouse?

• How has Christ encouraged you together this week?

Pray Together

Renuzit

Proverbs 4:18

"The path of righteousness is like the first gleam of dawn,
shining ever brighter till the full light of day."

Renuzit — what a funny name! I suppose the manufacturer of this
product put together the words "Renews it," for that's what this little
can of air freshener does. Just a few squirts, and a musty, smelly room
is filled with a fresh, new aroma.

All marriages could use a little renewing now and then. Like the
first gleam of dawn that brings new life to each day, renewal brings
new hope and new beginnings to the daily routine of married life. Ask
God today to bless your marriage with a fresh new outlook.

Marriage Moments:

• What part of your marriage could use a little renewal today?

• How will you make it happen?

Pray Together

78

Running On Reserve

1 John 4:19

"We love because he first loved us."

My car has a reserve fuel tank. When the warning light on the fuel gauge comes on, I know I have fifty miles of fuel left. I'm thankful for this warning light; it reminds me that it's time to refuel and helps to keep me from being stranded on the highway.

I've discovered that I need a reserve supply of love for my marriage relationship. Sometimes I get so depleted of energy and emotion that there seems to be nothing left to give my wife. That's when I switch to my reserve supply. It is there I find that deep, satisfying love that is the very foundation of our relationship. It is this love that keeps me going and keeps our marriage strong and secure.

Marriage Moments:

- Do you have a "reserve tank" built into your marriage?

- How often do you tap into your reserves? How do you get them refilled?

Pray Together

Resident Or President

Ezekiel 36:27

"And I will put my Spirit in you and move you to follow my
decrees and be careful to keep my laws."

There's a big difference between living in a nation and being the
leader of that nation. Residents abide . . . presidents guide. One just
lives, the other must give.

Spiritually, many of us never allow the Holy Spirit to be the
president of our marriage relationships, only a resident within our self-
controlled walls. To reach our full potential — individually and as a
couple — we must allow the Holy Spirit to have complete control of
our lives. The surrender of our own agendas and our self-will can be
painful, but it brings great joy and blessing. Once He is president, life
will never be the same.

Marriage Moments:

- Does the Holy Spirit simply abide or is He the guide in your
  individual lives and your marriage relationship?

- What do you need to yield to Him?

Pray Together

R-E-S-P-E-C-T

1 Peter 2:17a

"Show proper respect to everyone."

I confess, there are times when I don't show proper respect to my wife. Sometimes I do it on purpose, other times without thinking. Every time I betray her confidence, undermine her authority or am indifferent to her needs, I have acted foolishly and without sensitivity.

When she needs to talk, I should listen. When she needs to cry, I should hold her. When she needs to be left alone, I should walk away. When she is tired, I should allow her to rest. My wife is my greatest treasure. I must treat her the way I would want to be treated, for after all, she is a part of me.

Marriage Moments:

- Do you intentionally frustrate and exasperate your spouse? If so, why?

- Establish disciplinary measures that you must follow when you are disrespectful to each other.

Pray Together

Throw Him A Rope

Psalm 73:26

"My flesh and my heart may fail, but God is the strength
of my heart and my portion forever."

Jim Moore shares the following story in the July-September 1995
issue of *Homiletics* magazine.

Two scientists were on a field trip in the mountains. They
discovered a baby eagle in a nest on a jutting rock, just below the top
of a dangerous cliff. The eaglet had been deserted, and they wanted to
rescue it. They asked the young son of their guide if they could lower
him on a rope to fetch the little bird.

The boy was not at all enthusiastic about their plan, so he declined.
They offered him money, then doubled it, but still the boy refused.

Finally, one of the scientists asked in despair: "Well, then, how are
we going to save the baby eagle?"

The young boy replied: "I'd be glad to go down to rescue the bird
for free if you'll let my dad hold the rope."

God is the holder of the rope. He is the One who sustains life and
keeps His children from falling. I trust Him to hold me as I seek to be
the servant of my marriage and my family.

Marriage Moments:

- In what way have you allowed Christ to hold the rope of your
  marriage?

- In what way have you sought to hold it yourselves? Pray to give
  it over to Him.

Pray Together

Believing Is Seeing

2 Peter 1:8

"For if you possess these qualities in increasing measure,
they will keep you from being ineffective and unproductive
in your knowledge of our Lord Jesus Christ."

We've all heard the phrase "seeing is believing." It means that the proof is in the visual — I see it, therefore I believe it. How about turning it around? If we're willing to believe in each other, we will begin to see each other as God sees us. Our effectiveness and productiveness for Christ will increase as we encourage and support one another.

Believing in each other means that we will focus on the potential and not the problems. Possibilities will replace imperfections. Encouragement will replace criticism. Positive attitudes will push away negative ones. And we will see what was there all along — a person of beauty and worth.

Marriage Moments:

• What does Christ see in your marriage partner?

• How could you better affirm these beautiful qualities and attributes in each other?

Pray Together

Is She Here Yet?

Colossians 3:18

"Wives, submit to your husbands, as is fitting in the Lord."

The feminist movement has misinterpreted the art of submission. Feminists would have women believe that to submit is to lose all their identity in order to be dominated by men. But submission is an act of extreme love for another person. Consider our example, Jesus Christ. His act of total submission on the cross was the ultimate display of love. Every time we follow His example by putting others first, we please Him. Notice that our verse says submission is "fitting in the Lord."

I am honored that my wife trusts me to lead our household. She is my helper, my supporter and my biggest fan. When I'm speaking, I love to know that she's in the audience. It gives me a special thrill to know she is thinking of me and praying for me.

The wife who is a source of encouragement and strength for her husband will find herself elevated and honored, and her marriage will prosper.

Marriage Moments:

- As a wife, do you honor and support your husband? How?

- As a husband, do you take time to thank your wife and ask the Lord to bless her?

Pray Together

A Shotgun Start

Psalm 149:16

"Sing to the Lord a new song."

Once each year, I play in a golf outing where foursomes (four member groups) of golfers are positioned at each individual hole on the course. After everyone has been given time to get in the appropriate location, a shotgun blast occurs at the clubhouse and each group begins to play. The obvious purpose is to get everyone participating at once without long delays on the first tee.

Occasionally, I think we need to use the same approach to marriage growth. What is it that would jolt you and me into a fresh start — a departure from the humdrum? Why not let each day be a new beginning — full of songs of praise to the One who is the author of new life?

Marriage Moments:

• Is your marriage in need of a spark to keep you moving?

• What would that motivation be? How will you seek it?

Pray Together

Spacing Out

Proverbs 4:26

"Make level paths for your feet and take
only ways that are firm."

Have you ever arrived at your destination without remembering the trip? Your mind was elsewhere; you were not focused on your surroundings. Unfortunately, you missed seeing all the beautiful scenery along the way.

It's easy to put marriage on auto-pilot, too. We float along, thinking about other things, when we're suddenly jolted back to reality. Then we wonder what happened — why have we lost communication with each other and what did we do wrong?

The answer is that we spaced-out. We didn't pay attention to the details of marriage and we've missed all the little moments that make married life wonderful.

Don't let it happen to you! Take time each day to appreciate your spouse and keep focused on your surroundings. Enjoy the trip!

Marriage Moments:

- Do you "space out" often in your marriage? Does this occur when your spouse is talking to you?

- Is your marriage boring? Why or why not?

Pray Together

86

Speed Limit – 55

Galatians 5:22-23

"But the fruit of the Spirit is love, joy, peace, patience, kindness, goodness, faithfulness, gentleness and self control. Against such things there is no law."

Even though there are times we don't want to obey the signs, speed limits are designed to protect us on the highways. Sometimes we get frustrated when the speed limit requires us to go much slower than seems necessary. But we understand these rules are for our own safety.

Marriage has some "speed limit" signs that are nothing more than good principles to live by to keep the relationship safe. Consider these limits: 1) Life-long commitment, 2) Faithfulness, 3) Honesty, 4) Fellowship. If these rules are ignored, the relationship will suffer from an accident. We see it occurring around us every day. Though these God-given limits can often seem dull and boring, they were set in place for the good of marriage — to keep it harmonious and pure and holy.

Marriage Moments:

- What rules have proved very important in your relationship?

- If you chose to break God's rules, what would be the consequences for your marriage?

Pray Together

If At First You Don't Succeed

Deuteronomy 30:9b

"The Lord will again delight in you and make you prosperous,
just as he delighted in your fathers."

There's an unspoken rule in our society which says: "Go to college, study hard, graduate with a degree and have a successful life. This is the only way to get ahead." Certainly we need to prepare ourselves for the future, but is there more to success than merely being successful?

God doesn't base our success on the number of diplomas hanging on the wall. In fact, no matter our age or level of education, God views us as successful if we are willing to go wherever He leads. If you feel unfulfilled, evaluate your desire to be in the center of God's will. Contentment can only come when you are where He wants you to be.

MARRIAGE MOMENTS:

- From God's view, are you successful? Why or why not?

- How could you move more toward the center of God's will?

PRAY TOGETHER

This Is A Pain

Psalm 119:153

"Look upon my suffering and deliver me."

I have several friends whose spouses suffer intense physical and emotional pain because of ailments or diseases. Every time I visit them I have a new appreciation for the grace and love they show each other. The reason they suffer is often unclear, but their example is a good reminder of the fact that Christ's love is stronger than any pain and more enduring than any suffering.

During times of suffering, seek to be a source of strength for your marriage partner. Discover what you can do to bring joy and comfort to the one you love.

Marriage Moments:

- Who do you know that shows Christ's love through their suffering? Pray for them.

- How can you be more sensitive to your spouse during times of difficulty and pain?

Pray Together

Sweet Sleep

Proverbs 3:24

"When you lie down, you will not be afraid; when you lie down, your sleep will be sweet."

One of the delights of marriage is the privilege of snuggling up under the covers on a cold winter night. There's just something about the warmth of two bodies that brings peacefulness and sweet sleep.

When I am lying like this next to my wife, I experience a wonderful feeling of well-being. Our hearts and our hands are entwined. There is no fear, no anxiety, no mistrust. The next day may hold great struggles and pain, but for those few hours, everything is right with the world. What a marvelous gift from our Father!

Tonight, as you lie down, gently hold each other and experience sweet sleep.

Marriage Moments:

• What do you enjoy about your sleep and rest together?

• Could you cuddle more? Kiss more? Hold each other more?

Pray Together

Please Don't Take It Away

Proverbs 3:33

"The Lord's curse is on the house of the wicked,
but he blesses the home of the righteous."

Sometimes my children aren't very careful with their possessions. I often find myself saying, "Hey, be careful with that or I'll take it away!" I have tried to teach them to respect and appreciate their things. They know that without the proper care, toys become broken, clothes are torn and puppies get sick. Marriage ought to be handled in the same way — with care, appreciation and respect.

Look at a picture of you and your spouse. Imagine your relationship as a beautifully wrapped gift from God. It is a treasure of great value — one that requires the highest level of care. Now think of what your life might be like if this gift were taken away. Rejoice together and be thankful for God's goodness.

Marriage Moments:

- Using descriptive and thankful words, tell each other how grateful you are for the gift of your marriage.

- Have a new picture taken of you together and put it in a prime location in the house and/or office.

Pray Together

If You Don't Have It, Just Take It

Ephesians 6:10

"Be strong in the Lord and his mighty power."

A friend recently challenged me in a note with these thoughts.

> I pray that you will take time for your children, take time for your wife and take time for the Lord. Notice that it is TAKE time and not FIND time. If you're like me, that's the catch.

Isn't this true? If we want to build our relationships with loved ones, we must TAKE advantage of opportunities to do so. We must set dates on the calendar. We must keep appointments. We must not sit around, waiting for it to happen. We must — with the Lord's help — TAKE time.

Marriage Moments:

- How much time do you take to spend together daily? Weekly?

- If you had more time together, how would it benefit your marriage? Then do it!

Pray Together

92

Does Your Walk Match Your Talk?

Isaiah 33:15-16

"He who walks righteously and speaks what is right . . .
will dwell on the heights. . . . His bread will be
supplied, and water will not fail him."

As a public speaker, I find myself continually challenged to live at home the way I speak on stage. I've made a contract with my family. If they see inconsistencies between my walk and my talk, they have the right to confront me . . . and they have.

We all need to be held accountable for our words and our actions. If the "walk" doesn't match the "talk," we will appear dishonest and wishy-washy. But it is not always easy to do what is right, even though we preach it. How can we be persons of integrity, never compromising ourselves or our faith?

Our lives should be mirrors of Christ, who put into practice all the virtues He preached. Seek Him today and ask Him to fill you with the desire and the strength to be a person of character and honesty. Believe me, people will take notice!

Marriage Moments:

- Who holds you accountable for the words you say and the actions that follow?

- What actions can you take to improve your "walk" with your spouse?

Pray Together

I'm Ready Coach

1 Peter 1:13

"Therefore, prepare your minds for action; be self-controlled;
set your hope fully on the grace to be given you
when Jesus Christ is revealed."

In the early 1920s, the Texas A & M coach called a fan out of the stands to be prepared to play in case one of their eleven football players was injured. The anxious fan kept saying, "If you need me coach, I'm ready to play." Since then, the student section stands during each game as a statement to the coach that they are on the team and ready to play.

I want my wife to know I'm standing ready to help in any way I can. My mind is prepared for action. I'm glad to be part of the team.

Marriage Moments

- Is your spouse a team player? Is he or she ready and willing to support you?

- How could you better support each other?

Pray Together

94

The Box

Genesis 3:8

"The man and his wife heard the sound of the Lord God as he was walking in the cool of the day, and they hid from the Lord God among the trees of the garden."

My brother, Joe, and I used to perform a short magic show for small groups. We had two basic tricks and tried to make them last as long as possible. One trick included a special magic box that appeared to be empty, but, when positioned correctly, revealed a secret compartment filled with a long scarf.

When husbands and wives try to keep secrets from each other, the result can be disastrous. Marriage should be filled with honesty and truth, not deception. Adam and Eve found they could not hide from God, for He knew all about them. And He knows about us, too — our fears, our hurts, our past with all its mistakes.

Christ came to bring us freedom from those secrets which haunt us. Open your heart to Him today.

Marriage Moments:

- What are you hiding in your secret compartments?

- Share openly with your spouse and pray for healing in these areas.

Pray Together

Theme Words

Psalm 94:12-13

"Blessed is the man you discipline, O Lord, the man you teach from your law; you grant him relief from days of trouble, till a pit is dug for the wicked."

One practice we've enjoyed in our home is the adoption of theme words for ourselves. For example, my current word is "discipline." My wife and children constantly remind me that I need to be growing in this area of my life. They also have theme words like excellence, spirit, joy, hope and patience.

It's good practice to have a theme word. It gives a focus and direction to life. What would be a good theme word for your marriage? Faithfulness? Self-sacrificing? Spirit-filled?

Whatever theme word you set for yourselves, God can help you reach that goal. He can give you the right attitude and the strength you will need to change and grow. Trust in Him, for He is faithful.

Marriage Moments:

- What words would your friends use to describe your marriage?

- What word will you choose for personal development in your own life for the next two months?

Pray Together

King Of The Hill

Isaiah 40:29

"He gives strength to the weary and increases the
power of the weak."

David Robinson, an outspoken Christian and center for the San
Antonio Spurs professional basketball team, recently said, "It's easier
to defend the hill from the top than the bottom." He's right! When
you're at the top, you can see your opponent coming from all sides. At
the top, you have more confidence and self-assurance. At the top,
you're no longer scrambling, but defending.

I love the comment because it applies to marriage as well as
basketball. If our marriages are to be sturdy and grounded, we've
got to climb to the top of the hill. Too many couples are willing to
settle for the thrill of the foothills and miss the beauty of the view
from the top!

Marriage Moments:

• Where are you currently positioned on the "hill" of marriage?

• What have you done today to move toward the top?

Pray Together

My Top Ten

1 John 4:11

"Dear friends, since God so loved us, we also ought to love one another."

At their first counseling session, I ask engaged couples to give me ten reasons why they know marriage is "right" for them. It's amazing how many can't think of more than two or three, and even those are lame!

We don't think about these things often enough, do we? Can you list ten reasons why you're in love? I challenge you to try it. Do it together. Be thankful for those qualities in your spouse that first brought you together.

Marriage Moments:

- List ten reasons you're in love.

- Plan on sharing at least one reason each day this coming week. As reasons pop into your mind, verbalize them.

Pray Together

98

Trap Doors
Revelation 3:20

"Here I am! I stand at the door and knock. If anyone hears
my voice and opens the door, I will come in and eat
with him, and he with me."

Every day we encounter hundreds of doors. Most of us walk through three or more just going from one part of the house to the other. There are elevator doors, car doors, cabinet doors, restroom doors, garage doors and office doors. There are also figurative doors — doors of opportunity, service and advancement.

How do we know what lies beyond the door before us? Is it a door of opportunity or one of pain and frustration? Is Satan trying to trap us into opening the wrong door?

The key is to open the one "true door" that hinges on Jesus. He is waiting and knocking, hoping that you will let Him in. Both marriage partners need to make this decision in order for the partnership to be what Christ desires.

Marriage Moments:
•Have you opened the door of your hearts to receive Jesus Christ?

•If not, Read John 3:16 and John 1:12. Pray together for a new beginning in Christ.

Pray Together

The Triangle Principle

1 Corinthians 13:4a, 8a

"Love is patient, love is kind. Love never fails."

When a couple stands before the altar and says, "Till death do us part," they are acknowledging the fact that there might be pain and hard times ahead. One of the benefits of marriage is that there is a partner to share the joys as well as the sorrows. But sometimes husbands and wives fail to recognize each other's struggles. They lack patience and kindness, and the marriage begins to suffer.

In a relationship centered upon God, both spouses seek to grow more toward Him and eventually know each other completely through their knowledge of Him. Only through complete devotion to God can married couples find complete devotion to each other. He is the One who brings unity, patience, kindness and enduring love.

Marriage Moments:

• In what areas do you lack love and patience?

• What are you doing to seek unity in God? How have you grown closer this week?

Pray Together

100

Truth Decay

Ephesians 5:8

"For you were once darkness, but now you are light
in the Lord. Live as children of light."

God's Word is the definitive word of truth. If we aren't exposing ourselves to His truth and applying it to our lives, we should expect moral decay to occur. It takes discipline to stay focused on His Word. But how great are the rewards!

A marriage based on God's Word has a strong foundation that will withstand any storm and a peace that passes all understanding. Moral decay and corruption cannot touch it, for it is built on the solid rock of God's truth.

Take time today to begin increasing your understanding of the Word. Study it together. You will be amazed at its relevance and power!

Marriage Moments:

- Do you read the Bible together? How often?

- What passage has recently ministered to you and brought strength to your relationship?

Pray Together

God Allows U-Turns

Isaiah 17:7

"In that day men will look to their Maker and turn their
eyes to the Holy One of Israel."

I'd always been careful when it came to making U-turns on the
highway — I didn't want to get caught! That all changed when a
policeman told me it wasn't illegal in our state. In fact, if one checks
both ways, it's perfectly legal. Knowing this gave me renewed
freedom on the road.

Our verse in Isaiah refers to those who will witness the ruin of
Damascus. When the people see the hopelessness of the city and watch
its glory fade, then they will turn to their Maker.

Many married couples do the same thing. They wait until their
marriage is in ruins before turning to the One who can make them
whole again. Why not turn now instead of later? God allows U-turns.
Accept His offer of freedom and salvation and see the change He can
make in your lives.

Marriage Moments:

- How could a U-turn be helpful for you? What area of your
  marriage needs to be turned around?

- Pray that God will grant you both a willingness and a longing to
  be changed.

Pray Together

What You Crave

Genesis 3:16b

"Your desire will be for your husband."

During one of Jane's pregnancies, she had a constant craving for Granny Smith apples. Every evening around sundown she would make her way to the refrigerator to get that apple. She couldn't explain why. It was a need — a desire deep within her that would not be denied.

What do you crave in your marriage? Do you have a deep desire to be with your spouse, to share laughter and tears together? Do you crave intimacy? Do you want to grow together in the Lord and become more like Him? Ask God to help you fulfill each other's needs and desires, that your marriage may be both satisfying and full of anticipation.

Marriage Moments:

- What do you crave in your marriage relationship?

- Are any of your cravings detrimental to your marriage?

Pray Together

What'd You Say?

Colossians 3:17a

"Whatever you do, whether in word or deed, do it all
in the name of the Lord Jesus."

A friend of mine recently surveyed several couples to see what they
would do if they received a call saying surprise guests were coming to
their home for dinner. The women in the survey responded with details
about the preparation of the home and the food. The men saw it as an
opportunity to call for pizza delivery. The women planned a social
gathering with lots of class; the men planned to eat.

It's a fact — men and women are very different from each other. They
do not view life in the same way; neither do they respond alike to the world
around them. This difference causes problems for many marriages. But
husbands and wives should learn to appreciate these differences and be
sensitive to each other's needs. Of course, it takes practice. But a marriage
full of understanding and honest communication is worth the effort.

Marriage Moments:

- What would each of you do if you found out a surprise guest was
  coming for dinner? How are you alike and different in your
  reactions?

- From what you have learned about each other, how can you work
  together and individually to relate to each other?

Pray Together

Who Cares?

Psalm 55:22

"Cast your cares on the Lord and he will sustain you;
he will never let the righteous fall."

If I were honest, I would have to admit that there are times when I come home with an "I don't care" attitude. Jane begins sharing with me the events of her day, and I just let her talk. I am too tired to care.

In these times when I fail to give her the attention and support she deserves, I'm glad that she can find comfort in the loving arms of our Father. He is always standing ready to receive His children when they turn to Him. He always cares for us — we can count on it!

Marriage Moments:
- Share a specific time Christ provided strength for you when your spouse was unwilling or insensitive.

- Offer a prayer of thanksgiving to God for His unceasing strength.

Pray Together

Whoppertunities

2 Thessalonians 1:4

"Therefore, among God's churches we boast about
your perseverance and faith in all the persecutions
and trials you are enduring."

Paul constantly encouraged his fellow believers in the Lord.
Notice in today's verse how he says "we boast about you."   In
marriage, the importance of encouragement is obvious. People feel
better about themselves when they know they are appreciated, and they
respond more positively toward those who compliment them.

Do you want to see your spouse come alive and blossom before
your very eyes? Then find opportunities to give a "whopper" of a
compliment. Sincere praise can melt the hardest heart. Be a spouse
that boasts about your partner. Look for "whoppertunities" today.

Marriage Moments:

• Do you compliment your spouse privately and publicly?

• Take time to compliment several of your spouse's strengths
right now.

Pray Together

Worship

Psalm 100:2

"Worship the Lord with gladness; come before
him with joyful songs."

Every Sunday morning I look out at couples sitting across the congregation. They have spent the week together, sometimes in joy and other times in sorrow. I wonder how many of them are really worshipping and how many are just following tradition and ritual.

Worship is an opportunity for couples to come together for confession, adoration and praise. It is a chance for husbands and wives to be united with Christ and with other believers.

Let your worship become an occasion for great joy, not just another ritual to perform. It will solidify your relationship and bring you closer to God.

Marriage Moments:

- Do you worship together regularly? If not, when will you start?

- Do you discuss the scripture lessons and the message brought to you in worship? If not, why not? What could you learn if you were willing?

Pray Together

Zeke Leaks

Ezekiel 36:27

"And I will put my Spirit in you and move you to follow my decrees and be careful to keep my laws."

Dr. Ray Ortlund tells the story of a man named Zeke who always prayed, "Lord fill me up with Your Spirit." It was his consistent public prayer for many years. An individual who grew tired of this prayer approached the pastor and asked, "Why does Zeke keep praying to be filled with His Spirit?" The pastor responded, "That's easy . . . Zeke leaks!"

How true of all of us. We are drained, pulled, pushed and stretched in life — and especially in our marriage relationships. How long can we continue this pattern before communication becomes strained and marriages start to crumble? The joy and wonder of that relationship has "leaked" out and has left us with disillusionment and sadness. That is why we need God's Spirit to continually fill us. His love will seal up the holes and make us complete again.

Marriage Moments:

- What "leaks" are you experiencing in your marriage?

- Can the Holy Spirit bring renewal in these areas? Have you asked Him yet?

Pray Together

Always In Season

Leviticus 26:3-4a

"If you follow my decrees and are careful to obey my commands, I will send you rain in its season."

The changing of the seasons is truly one of God's greatest miracles. The freshness of spring, the warmth of summer, the beauty of fall and the icy winter — all proclaim His glory to the world.

Our lives experience seasons, too — seasons of joy, of sorrow, of great difficulty or great peace. You may be experiencing such a season at this time. Whatever the time of year or the time of life, remember that God's love is always in season. It never changes. It never fails. His love can be yours to strengthen your marriage and bring it into a season of maturity and great satisfaction.

Marriage Moments:

• What season best represents you today? Both of you?

• How have you helped each other during the icy winters?

Pray Together

The Best Interest Rate

Colossians 3:15-16

"Let the peace of Christ rule in your hearts. . . .
And be thankful. Let the word of Christ dwell in you
richly as you teach and admonish one another with all
wisdom, and as you sing psalms, hymns and spiritual
songs with gratitude in your hearts to God."

This passage gives five suggestions for keeping the best interest rate of your relationship a top priority:

1. LIVE AT PEACE. Bring a sense of calmness to the relationship.
2. BE THANKFUL. Pass on a word of appreciation to your spouse every day.
3. TEACH AND ADMONISH WITH GODLY WISDOM. Help each other grow; be willing to receive advice from your spouse.
4. SING TOGETHER. Keep a melodious spirit alive in the home.
5. DO EVERYTHING IN HIS NAME. Let your life and your marriage glorify God.

Practicing these scriptural principles will yield great dividends.

Marriage Moments:

• Evaluate these five areas in your relationship.

• How are you both investing in the relationship and what dividends have you seen?

Pray Together

The Boomerang Principle

Philippians 4:8

"... Whatever is admirable ... think about such things."

In the original Greek text, the word "admirable" means "things fit for God to hear." I often wonder if people think that God can't hear their conversations. How different would their choice of words be if they could see God standing beside them?

Consider implementing the boomerang principle into your lifestyle. Treat every word that flows out of your mouth as if it were coming back to you. You can be sure that speaking those "admirable" words will make a difference in your life. It will change the way you talk to your spouse. You will begin to feel better about yourself and your relationship with God will reach a new level. Try it today!

Marriage Moments:

- If the words you've said this week came back to you, how would you feel?

- What phrases do you love to hear about yourself? How and when will you use them to compliment your spouse?

Pray Together

A Mountain Of Distractions

Proverbs 6:23b-24

"The corrections of discipline are the way to life, keeping you from the immoral woman, from the smooth tongue of the wayward wife."

There are so many potential distractions to marriage. Satan is a master at manipulation; he specializes in pitting husbands and wives against each other. He uses commonplace things — other people, job pressures, the children — to build a mountain between marriage partners.

Seek God's wisdom that you will recognize these distractions and His strength that you will be able to resist them. Talk about them together and pray about them every day. Allowing a mountain of distractions to grow between you and your spouse will cause your relationship to deteriorate.

Marriage Moments:

• What distractions are facing you individually and as a couple?

• Discuss practical ways to work together and address the distractions.

Pray Together

112

Get Into The Groove

Philippians 4:8

". . . Whatever is noble . . . think about such things."

The Greek word for noble is "semnos." It is used to describe a man or woman who moves throughout the world as though it were the sanctuary of God.

It is easy to walk out of a sanctuary or place of prayer and move into a different state of mind — one that isn't worshipful. Life has a way of knocking us out of that groove in which we desire to stay.

In today's verse, Paul challenges us to view all the world as a sanctuary. Everything is under God's canopy — the home, the car, the job — and nothing is outside His reach. What an invitation to excellence! Will you answer the call?

Marriage Moments:

• Do you treat your home as though it were the sanctuary of God?

• What can you do to make your home more of a place of worship?

Pray Together

Simply The Best

Matthew 18:3

"Except you change and become like little children,
you will never enter the kingdom of heaven."

I often think about the childlike characteristics that tend to slip away from us as we "mature" into adulthood: innocence . . . trust . . . forgiveness . . . unconditional love . . . happiness . . . simplicity . . . honesty. What happens to these characteristics as we grow older?

Living the simple life is still the best option. By the time most people figure this out, it is too late to do anything about it. Don't let it happen to you. Take time today to evaluate your lifestyle. Are there ways to simplify things and enjoy more time together? How can you recapture some of the joys of childhood? Spend time with God as you seek a simpler life together.

Marriage Moments:

- Share with your spouse one of your most enjoyable moments as a child. Why was it so much fun?

- Discuss one practical thing you could do to simplify your life.

Pray Together

114

Laying Down Our Weapons

James 4:1

"What causes fights and quarrels among you? Don't they come from your desires that battle within you?"

Marriage brings battles. It *is* normal. These battles can vary from a slingshot of words to a shotgun blast of criticism. They occur because one or both partners are dealing with inner struggles or selfish motives, or perhaps they have allowed themselves to be swayed by the natural tendency toward evil.

Daily submission to God and a genuine desire for His guidance, as recommended in James 4:7-10, is the solution to these marriage wars. God is the great giver of peace. With His help, we can declare a cease-fire and lay down our weapons.

Marriage Moments:

- What weapons do you use in your marriage relationship? Actions? Attitudes? Words?

- Ask the Lord daily to bring a cease-fire to your inner battles. Share these struggles with each other and pray together for the Lord's direction and strength.

Pray Together

Unbreakable

Ecclesiastes 4:12

"Though one may be overpowered, two can defend themselves.
A cord of three strands is not quickly broken."

At a wedding, I watched the bride and groom weave a cord of three strands as part of the ceremony. The three strands stood for the three people in the relationship — the bride, the groom and Christ. Woven together, they symbolized the strength of their marriage. It was a unique way to express their love for each other and for Christ.

The process of weaving needs to continue as time passes. The three strands must always be present — the husband, the wife and Christ — in order for the cord to be strong. The cord of marriage will feel many tugs, but with God's help, it will remain unbroken. May God bless you as you work to make your marriage a thing of strength and beauty.

Marriage Moments:

- What are you doing to weave a closer relationship?

- Is your relationship strong enough to handle the struggles ahead? How can you make it stronger?

Pray Together

Personal Journal . . .

Ephesians 5:22-32

This passage is the ultimate passage about a marriage
relationship. To understand it is to understand
God's love for each of us and our marriage.

- Specific lessons God is teaching us . . .

_____

_____

_____

_____

_____

_____

_____

_____

- Areas to continue to grow . . .

_____

_____

_____

_____

_____

_____

_____

_____

Establishing Our Future Goals . . .

- What do we want our marriage relationship to "look like" in one year.

_____

_____

_____

_____

_____

_____

- How will we accomplish this goal?

1._____

_____

2._____

_____

3._____

_____

4._____

_____

5._____

_____

Other Resources by Dan Seaborn & Winning At Home

DVD's
The Necessary Nine – *Nine ingredients that will make every marriage win!*
Strike A Match – *Remembering the spark that started your relationship and how to keep it burning.*
Brick By Brick – *Building a solid family – from the foundation up!*
Moses & The Ark – *What did Moses parents do? Why have we never thought about them?*
Keeping All Your Eggs In One Basket – *How to keep your family going in the same direction – toward God!*
Champions At Home – *The simple things we can do to honor God and love our family.*

VIDEOS
Brick by Brick – *Building a solid family – from the foundation up!*
Moses & The Ark – *What did Moses parents do? Why have we never thought about them?*
Keeping All Your Eggs In One Basket – *How to keep your family going in the same direction – toward God!*

CD's
Ten Ways Grandpa Said "I Love You" – *A personal reflection on the things Dan's grandpa did that impacted his life in a huge way! Laugh and cry as you relate.*
I Do…Cherish You – *What our wedding vows really mean.*
Single Parents & Other Biblical Heroes – *Encouragement for single parents.*

BOOKS
26 Words That Will Improve the Way You Do Family – *Simple parental ideas to help guide your family.*
One-Minute Devotionals for Couples – *Learn to pray together. It's "marriage" changing.*
Will You Hold Me? – *Devotional thoughts for parents.*
101 Ways to Love Your Wife – *Simple thoughts for ways to encourage your wife.*
101 Ways to Love Your Husband – *Simple thoughts for ways to encourage your husband.*
101 Ways to Improve at Dadhood – *Simple thoughts for ways to encourage your kids.*
101 Ways to Be an Awesome Kid – *Simple thoughts for ways to be a great kid.*

To order:
Visit www.winningathome.com OR
Call Winning At Home 1-800-772-7202

Winning At Home
Core Belief and Vision

To see people around the world experience the joy of their family and to win at home by loving each other and honoring Christ.

Dan has been gifted and impassioned to share his heart with a practical, humorous, and biblically sound approach. Through media outlets such as radio, seminars, conventions, television and corporations, families are experiencing the joy of *winning at home*.

*On every grave marker I've ever seen there's a birth date, a dash and a death date. The birth and death dates are important, but that little dash in the middle represents the mark you'll make with your life. The question I ask people is: "**What are you doing with your dash to impact your family?**" Each day, we have the privilege of adding to that dash. Before the dash is completed, we need to define our beliefs and live those out so our life will leave an awesome mark on our family.*

...Dan Seaborn

IN BALANCING HOME LIFE,
WINNING ISN'T EVERYTHING,
IT'S THE ONLY THING

Winning At Home
www.winningathome.com
1-800-772-7202